Everyday Prayers and Poems for Children

Dr Foyeke Christiana Tolani

Foreword by Rob Evans, The Donut Man

Published by PubliciseJesus Ltd. Oxford. United Kingdom.

PubliciseJesus Ltd books can be purchased in bulk for educational, children and youth groups, fundraising or sales for promotional use.

For more information, please email **admin@publicisejesus.org**

To contact the author, please email **ftolani@gmail.com**

A catalogue record for this book is available from the British Library.

Cover design by Amy Stokes

Typeset & design by Kafui Afenyo, Oxford UK (www.kafmedia.com)

ISBN 9780956839572

www.publicisejesus.com

Printed in Malta by Melita Press

PUBLICISE JESUS

To ______________________

From ______________________

Date ______________________

Dedication

This book is dedicated to my parents – Mr Emmanuel and Mrs Caroline Opaleye (who taught me how to pray); my children – Esther and Timothy Tolani; as well as all the children in the church (RCCG, Christ's Love Assembly, Oxford), I co-pastor with my husband (whose positive childlike traits I continually learn from.)

May God always be with you all and bless you abundantly.

THANK
YOU

Acknowledgements

I thank God for the inspiration and grace to write this book. Almighty God, may Your name be praised forever! I also thank my husband, Patrick Tolani (Senior Pastor, Redeemed Christian Church of God (RCCG), Christ's Love Assembly, Oxford for his love, support and encouragement. My gratitude also goes to the following people who kindly reviewed the book: Rob Evans (The Donut Man); Pastor Mary McCauley (National Director, RCCG Teenage Ministry, UK); Pastor Denrele Runsewe (National Director, RCCG Children's Ministry, UK); Andrea Onduku and Dr Afua Adu-Boateng.

Sincere appreciation also to Andrew Halloway and Susanna Blackmore who painstakingly edited and proofread the book, respectively. Lastly, I thank Mrs Bibianah Adedoyin, all my family members, in-laws, friends, and members of RCCG, Christ's Love Assembly, Oxford for their prayer and love.

May God bless you all beyond your imaginations, in Jesus' name. Amen.

Commendations

"I am excited about this beautiful prayer book that is comprehensive, simple and portrays that children can talk to God and pray about anything. It is also educational and transformational, it can help children develop good "Father God - Child" relationships and build them up as intercessors. I wish I had had this when I was a child. The prayers are crafted in a way that teaches children to be grateful, caring and mindful Christians. I highly recommend it for every child."

- **Pastor Mary McCauley** *(National Director, Teenage Ministry, Redeemed Christian Church of God, UK.)*

"This prayer book is definitely a need for all parents, guardians of children and all children. We are in a season when we have to pray. There are challenges in the society, a decay of moral values, uncertainty, fear and things seemingly going out of control. This book addresses the basics and fundamentals of prayer, a real and practical prayer book. The author gets to the heart of the matter. A must have for all family units, churches and schools."

- **Pastor Denrele Runsewe** *(National Director, Children's Ministry, Redeemed Christian Church of God, UK.)*

“This beautiful book is filled with prayers for every scenario and so children will never be stuck for words again. I also believe that the book will encourage children to articulate and express their feelings to God when they feel happy, sad, apologetic, or wanting to make better choices and their vocabulary is limited. The prayers are so simple and phrased in such a way that it seems they came straight from a child’s heart. This is a brilliant resource for children that will provide a wonderful foundation for a great relationship with their Saviour from an early age.”

- **Andrea Onduku** *(Director, Matters of the Heart Ministry, Bradford, UK. www.mattersofheart.org)*

“This is a great resource for both family and children’s personal prayer time. Some of the contents would also appeal to grown-ups who would like to come to God in prayer with childlike simplicity!”

- **Dr. Afua Adu – Boateng** *(Children’s Sunday School Teacher, Wolverhampton, UK.)*

“These delightful prayers are simple enough for children to use, yet profound enough to teach children more about Jesus. They are both personal and a thoughtful introduction to biblical teaching on prayer. The book is arranged in helpful themes which mirror children’s feelings and routines. I would use these prayers with my own children as they grow up.”

- **Susanna Blackmore** *(Proof Reader, Oxford, UK.)*

Foreword

Foyeke Tolani is a lovely, gentle Christian who loves Jesus, her church, her children Esther and Timothy, and now your family... with this, her book of prayers and poems for children. Here are prayers for every situation that a parent and child might face together, in words that beautifully convey and foster an inner life of simple trust and love of God. It is a Christian resource by which you and your children will find comfort and delight.

I had the privilege of working with Foyeke when she and her husband Patrick hosted my wife Shelley and me as I shared my 'Donut Man' ministry in their church. I found them both to shine with a passion and professionalism that is genuine; which was encouraging to me and I am sure, to all who have the blessing of knowing them. I commend Foyeke, her fine family and this wonderful book of prayers and poems to you and to the entire body of Christ.

Sincerely,
Rob Evans, The Donut Man
rob@donutman.com

Introduction

Direct your children onto the right path, and when they are older, they will not leave it. Proverbs 22:6 NLT

But Jesus said, "Let the children come to me. Don't stop them! For the Kingdom of Heaven belongs to those who are like these children." Matthew 19:14 NLT

Clearly the Bible is informative about many things, particularly the need for children to have special time in prayer and fellowship with God and to pray in Jesus' name; as well as the responsibility of parents to direct children on the right path - on which, prayer is key. John Chrysostom, a notable Christian bishop, said, "Prayer is the root, the fountain, the mother of a thousand blessings." Thus it is important to teach our children how to pray so that it becomes their lifestyle. This will ensure that their confidence is in the true God and they seek help from Him, whether they are with their parents or not.

This book has 70 inspired new prayers for different situations relating to children in the 21st century. You can read it to your child, or encourage your child to read it alone and use it as a guide in prayer. They can also memorise prayers to pray for themselves, the world, their friends and family.

It is worth mentioning that some prayers make mention of mothers at times and fathers at other times. These words can be used interchangeably. “His /her” when used in the text can also be used interchangeably to suit each child’s situation.

I pray that every child who uses this book will remain in Christ for the rest of their lives, growing to be a delightful and highly blessed child of God, in Jesus’ name. AMEN.

Table of Contents

Chapter 1

Thanksgiving Prayers

God's Goodness

1.

You are good, Lord

I will always come to you in prayers
You hear our requests and answer our prayers
You heal us, protect us, provide for us and forgive us
Thank you, Lord, for your goodness and kindness
Thank you, Lord, for everything.

2.

Thank you

"Say thank you" is a phrase I hear so many times
"Say thank you" for the sweets, food, clothes and presents
"Thank you" helps me show appreciation.
So I should thank you, Father God
Thank you for loving me just as I am
Thank you for forgiving me all my wrongdoing
Thank you for giving me a good family
Thank you for friends and all I have
Thank you, Father God, for everything.

3.

I'm blessed, Lord

I'm blessed, Lord, because you say so
Blessed in the morning
Blessed in the afternoon
Blessed in the evening
Blessed in every season
Blessed at home
Blessed in school
Blessed in the church
Blessed when I'm out and about
Lord I'm blessed, and this is all because of you
You love me so much and made me a blessed child
May I continue to be blessed and be a blessing
In Jesus' name I pray. Amen.

4.

Angels watching over me
Thank you, Lord, for angels
Especially the one assigned to me
Thank you, Lord, for angels
May they keep watching over me
Thank you, Lord, for angels
May they also watch over my
family and friends
Thank you, Lord.

Gifts

5.

Toys and games

Thank you for my toys and games
They keep me company
They are so delightful
What can I do without them?
But most importantly,
what would I do if you had not blessed me
With wonderful people who bought them for me?
Thank you, Lord, for my toys and
those who gave them to me
Thank you, Lord.

God's Creation

6.

A great God
How great God is
He made the moon, sun and stars
He made the sea, sky and land
He made the flowers, birds and animals
He made everything beautiful
Best of all, He amazingly and wonderfully made me!
How great God is
Thank you, Lord, for your greatness.

7.

Thank you for our beautiful world
Thank you, Lord, for all the beautiful things in our world
Beautiful flowers, that come in different colours
Different shapes, feels and lovely smells
Thank you, Lord, for all beautiful things
Beautiful animals, small and big, patterned and striped
Crawling and walking, climbing and jumping
All these things are so amazing
Thank you, Lord, for our beautiful world.

8.

Each little flower that blossoms

Each little flower that blossoms is a gift from you
Each bee that hums and bird that sings
Each blade of grass that grows and produces seeds for food
Each day that passes and we go through
All a bundle of gifts from you
For all these we thank and bless you, oh Lord.

9.

All things bright and beautiful

The Lord God made them all
All things bright and wonderful
The Lord God made them all
The green grass, white and blue sky
Beautiful gardens, flying butterflies
Calm seasides and lovely beaches
The Lord God made them all
All things bright and beautiful
Thank you, Lord, for making them all.

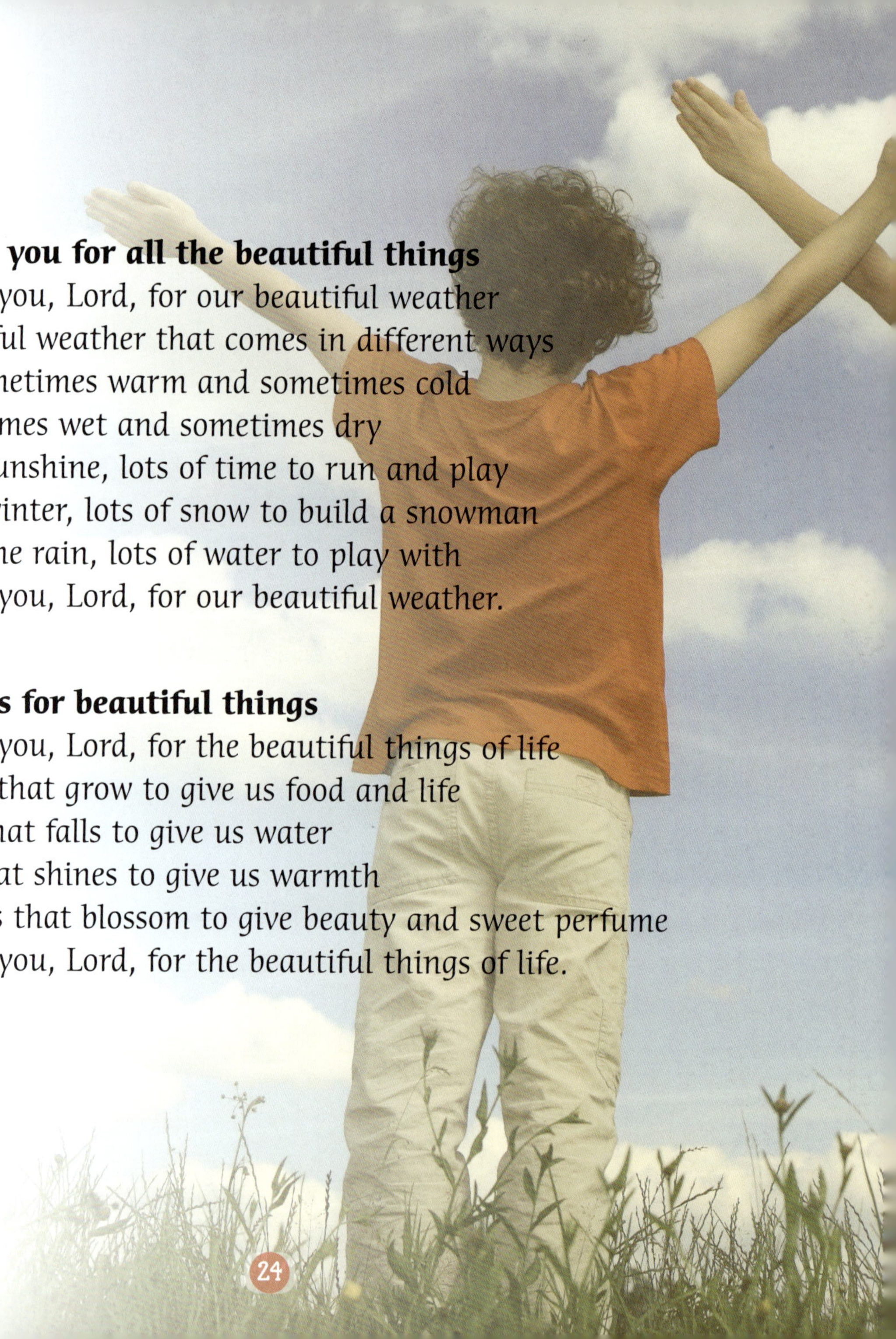

10.

Thank you for all the beautiful things

Thank you, Lord, for our beautiful weather
Beautiful weather that comes in different ways
It's sometimes warm and sometimes cold
Sometimes wet and sometimes dry
I like sunshine, lots of time to run and play
I like winter, lots of snow to build a snowman
I like the rain, lots of water to play with
Thank you, Lord, for our beautiful weather.

11.

Thanks for beautiful things

Thank you, Lord, for the beautiful things of life
Plants that grow to give us food and life
Rain that falls to give us water
Sun that shines to give us warmth
Flowers that blossom to give beauty and sweet perfume
Thank you, Lord, for the beautiful things of life.

12.

Thank you for everybody

Thank you, Lord, for everybody
The farmer that plants the food we eat
The police service that brings order to our city
The doctors and nurses who take care of us when we are sick
The teachers in school and church who teach us what is good
The neighbours and family friends who often keep
us company
The shopkeeper who sells toys and food to us
There are so many helpful people in this world
Thank you, Lord, for everybody.

Chapter 2

Daily Prayers

Morning

13.

It's a new day, Lord
How wonderful to see this new day
Thank you for a good night's rest
Sweet dreams and new strength for today
Thank you for the streaming light that marks the dawn
Thank you, Lord, for this new day
Kindly be with me today, in Jesus' name.

14.

Be with me
Be with me today, oh Lord
As I go to school and attend my classes
Help me to listen attentively and do my work carefully
Help me to be of good behaviour and obey instructions
Let me also be helpful to others and not be a bully
All these I ask for in Jesus' name. Amen.

Meals

15.

Bless this food, oh Lord
Sweet smells, mouth-watering tastes
Yummy cookies, nice meals
All plentiful gifts from you, oh Lord
Gifts provided by my parents through you
Thank you, Lord, for my food
Bless this food, oh Lord, in Jesus' name.

Family

16.

My family
I thank you, Lord, for my family members
Thank you for those who care for me
Bless them all in Jesus' name (daddy, mummy, granny etc)
Let them not be angry with me, dear Lord
Please be with us, guide us, and keep us from all evil
Provide for all our needs and let your love be with and in us.
In Jesus' name I pray. Amen.

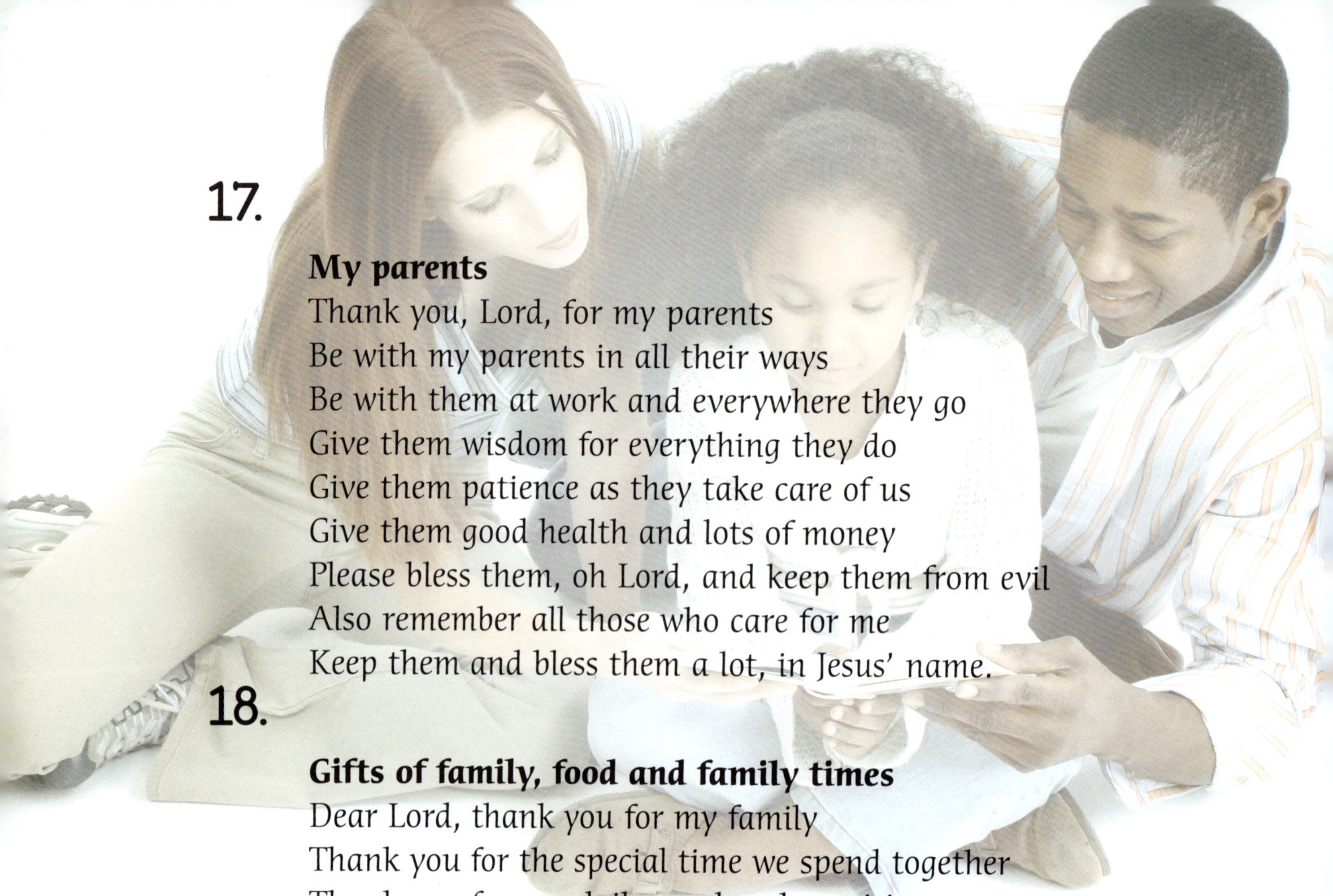

17.

My parents

Thank you, Lord, for my parents
Be with my parents in all their ways
Be with them at work and everywhere they go
Give them wisdom for everything they do
Give them patience as they take care of us
Give them good health and lots of money
Please bless them, oh Lord, and keep them from evil
Also remember all those who care for me
Keep them and bless them a lot, in Jesus' name.

18.

Gifts of family, food and family times

Dear Lord, thank you for my family
Thank you for the special time we spend together
Thank you for our daily meal and provisions
Thank you for the joy we share and peace in our home
Thank you, Lord, for our meal -
let it give health to our bodies
Thank you, Lord, for everything
Please remember those who do not have food and family
Provide for them, in Jesus' name.

Play Time

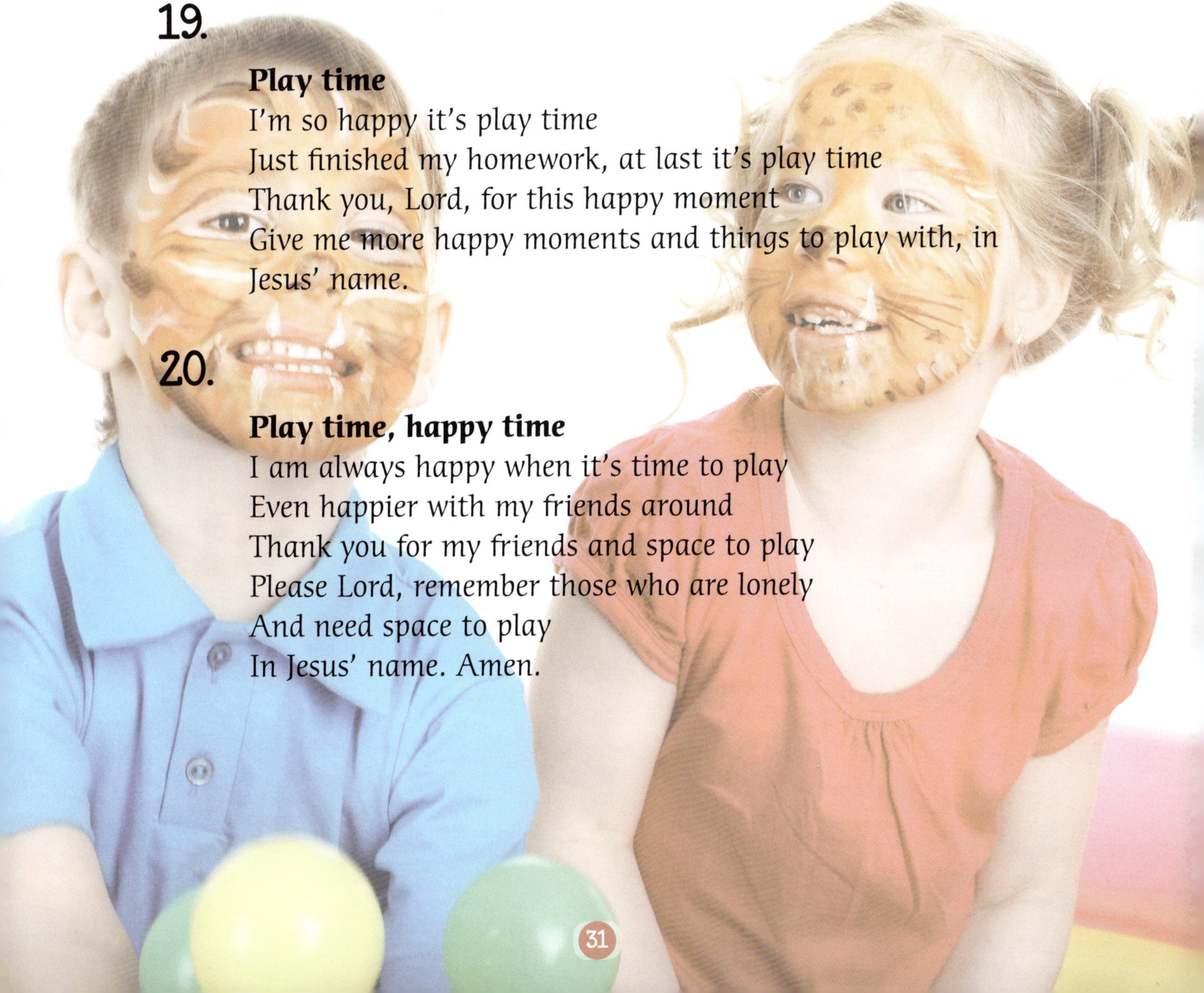

19.

Play time
I'm so happy it's play time
Just finished my homework, at last it's play time
Thank you, Lord, for this happy moment
Give me more happy moments and things to play with, in Jesus' name.

20.

Play time, happy time
I am always happy when it's time to play
Even happier with my friends around
Thank you for my friends and space to play
Please Lord, remember those who are lonely
And need space to play
In Jesus' name. Amen.

21.

Full of energy
Oh Lord, you strengthen me
I can jump, shout, scream and play
I'm told you give strength to the weak
Joy to the sad and satisfaction to the needy
Thank you, Lord, for everything
Especially the space to play and be happy.

Anytime

22.

Household chores
Mummy says "keep your room tidy"
Mummy says "pack up the toys"
Mummy says "do your homework"
Mummy says "put dirty clothes in one place"
Dear Lord, I know you want me to be good and helpful too
But sometimes I'm not, please forgive me.
Help me to be good, nice and helpful in Jesus' name.

23.

What a friend!
What a friend we have in Jesus
All our cares on him to lay
What a friend we have in Jesus
I can pour my heart to him
What a friend we have in Jesus
I can tell him all my needs
What a friend we have in Jesus
He is always there to listen
Thank, you, Lord for being my friend.

Night

24.

Now the day is over
Night is drawing near
The sun is setting, the light is fading
The moon is rising, the stars are coming out
I can hear “Go brush your teeth and put on your pyjamas!”
I know the next thing is to read my Bible and pray
Dear Lord,
Be with me and keep me from all evil
Let me sleep peacefully, in Jesus’ name.

25.

Thank you, Lord, for today
I have had such a wonderful day
A good warm bath
Breakfast, lunch and dinner
Lots of fun and activities as well
Thank you, Lord, for today
May I have a good night’s sleep, in Jesus’ name.

All the Time

26.

Our Father in heaven

Our Father in heaven may your name be kept holy
May your Kingdom come soon
May your will be done on earth, as it is in heaven.
Give us today the food we need
and forgive us our sins
as we have forgiven those who sin against us.
And don't let us yield to temptation
but rescue us from the evil one.
- Matthew 6:9b-13 (NLT)

27.

The Grace

The grace of our Lord Jesus Christ
The love of God
And the sweet fellowship of the Holy Spirit
Be with us now and for evermore. Amen.
- 2 Corinthians 13:14 (paraphrased)

28.

God's goodness

Surely goodness and mercy
Shall follow me
All the days of my life
And I will dwell in the house of the Lord
Forever and ever. Amen.
- Psalm 23:6 (paraphrased)

29.

All time blessings

Dear Lord,
Let Your light shine on me
Let Your peace be all around me
Let Your love be in me
Let Your character be seen in me
Let Your beauty reflect in me
Let Your blessings be always mine
In Jesus' name I pray. Amen.

30.

Amazing God

God You are good
God You are kind
God You are lovely
God You are wonderful
God You are great
God You are so precious to me
Dear Father God, please be always near me
In Jesus' name I pray. Amen.

Chapter 3

Good Feeling and Behaviour Prayers

Good Behaviour

31.

Giving
Dear Father God, I have heard so much about giving
Everything we have is given to us
You gave us life so we are alive today
You gave us sunshine so we can have warmth
and plants can grow
You gave us strength so we can move about
You gave us a family so we are loved and not lonely
Above all you gave us your Son – Jesus Christ – to save us
from our sins
Please teach me how to give, and may I always give and not
be mean. In Jesus' name. Amen.

32.

The truth
The truth is good, this I know
The truth is good, it keeps me from trouble
The truth is good, because Mum always spots a lie
The truth is good, even the Bible tells me so
Dear Lord, please forgive all my lies
Help me to be truthful and honest at all times.

33.

I will trust in YOU

My birthday is soon and Christmas is near
My wish list grows by the day
I wonder if I will get all my presents
Oh Lord, please let me get all my presents
Bless all those who care for me
Bless my family and meet all our needs
Bless the needy and make them happy
Let me keep trusting you all the way.

34.

Clasping my hands

Mum taught me to pray with my hands
clasped and eyes shut
Mum says it will help me to concentrate
and not be distracted
I sometimes obey and sometimes disobey
But just now as I clasp my hands and close my eyes
I feel a sense of love for a loving God
Hear me as I pray now, oh Lord,
with clasped hands and closed eyes.

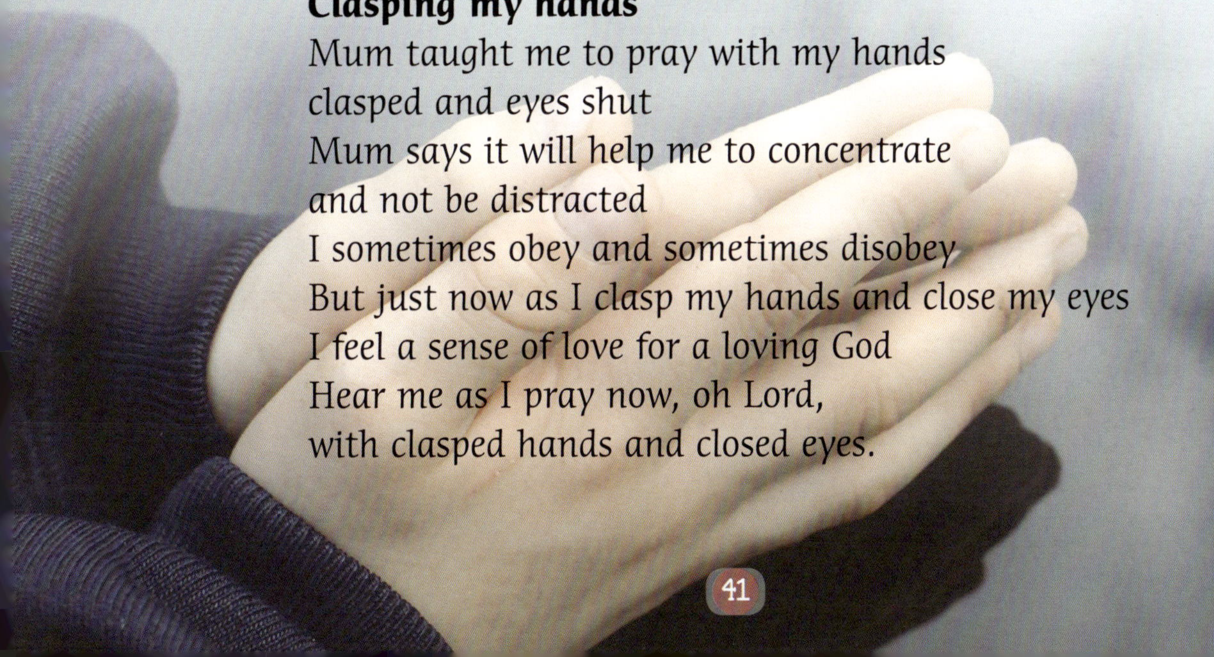

Good Aspirations

35.

When I grow up

When I grow up, I would like to be like Jesus
When I grow up, I would like to be great
When I grow up, I would like to be famous
When I grow up, I would like to be a celebrity
But Mum keeps saying I need to work hard in school first
Behave myself and be good
When I grow up, dear Lord,
please let me be the best I can possibly be
When I grow up, may I please you in all my ways.

36.

Being helpful

Jesus was helpful, I want to be helpful
Jesus was good, I want to be good
Jesus was obedient, I want to be obedient
Jesus was kind, I want to be kind
Jesus was hard-working,
I want to be hard-working and not lazy
Dear Father God, please help me to be like Jesus
In all I say and do.

37.

Be happy

Dear Lord, you want us to rejoice in you always
Help me to be happy and not sad
Help me to be thankful and always content
Help me to be grateful and always say thank you
When things don't happen my way or my family says NO
Still help me to be happy
Let me be happy all the time, in Jesus' name.

Chapter 4

Sad Feeling and Negative Attitude Prayers

Feeling Sorry

38.

The naughty corner

I don't like being here
Yet I'm here again
I am sorry, Lord
Will you forgive me?
Please forgive me, Lord
I will be good, in Jesus' name
Amen.

39.

Mistakes! Mistakes!

Lord, I've made another mistake
I am really so sorry
I really don't like to make mistakes or do bad things
Help me, Lord, to be good and do right
Mistakes, bad acts, you are not my friends
Help me, Lord, to always please you.

40.

Attitude
Sometimes I'm grumpy
Sometimes I'm dissatisfied
Sometimes I complain and can be rude
Sometimes I shout and get too cross
Sometimes I annoy my parents and others
But deep inside I know this is wrong
Even the Holy Bible tells me so
For all these wrongs, I ask for forgiveness
May I please you, Lord, and others from now on.

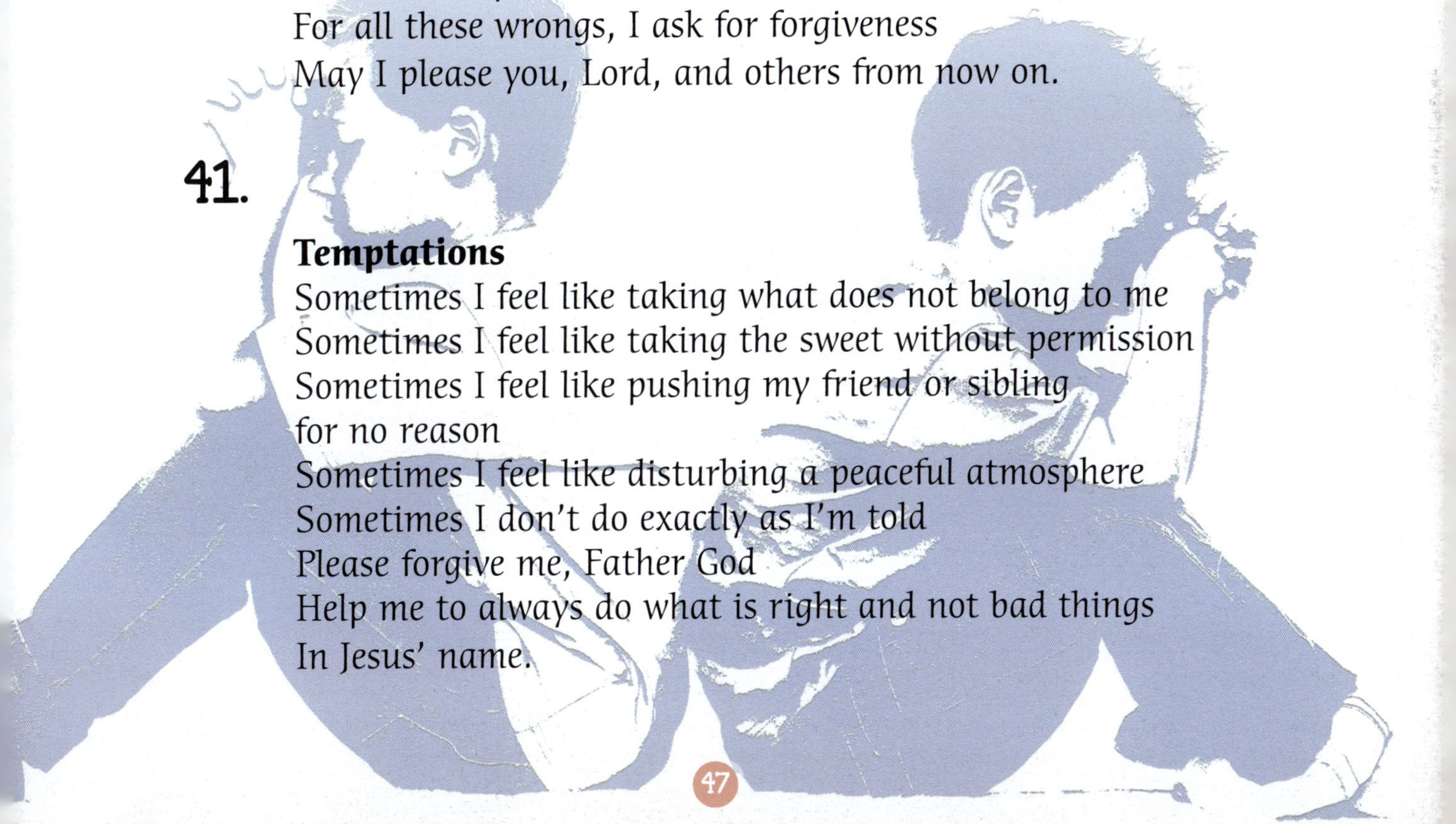

41.

Temptations
Sometimes I feel like taking what does not belong to me
Sometimes I feel like taking the sweet without permission
Sometimes I feel like pushing my friend or sibling
for no reason
Sometimes I feel like disturbing a peaceful atmosphere
Sometimes I don't do exactly as I'm told
Please forgive me, Father God
Help me to always do what is right and not bad things
In Jesus' name.

42.

Having my way

Dear Lord,
I sometimes want to have my way at all cost
I sometimes keep everything to myself
Sometimes too, I keep my sweets as well
Dear Lord, please help me to share and to be always nice
In Jesus' name I pray. Amen.

Feeling Fearful

43.

Afraid of the dark

Dear Lord, I am sometimes afraid of the dark and bad dreams
You taught us in the Holy Bible that you will give us sweet dreams
As I lie to sleep tonight, please grant me sweet dreams and good rest
May I not be afraid again, in Jesus' name. Amen.

44.

No need to fear
Help comes from God
No need to worry
God never fails
No need to panic
Everything will be all right
For help comes from God
And He is never too late.

45.

Fear? I will not fear
I'm told not to be afraid of the dark
Psalm 23 tells me so - 'Though I walk
Through the valley of the shadow of death
I will fear no evil, for you are with me.'
I will not be afraid of the scary tales and movies
The bullies lurking around the school corner
The creaks and scary sounds at night
I will trust in you, Lord, for you watch over me
Please keep watching over me and I will not fear.

Feeling Lonely

46.

When I'm lonely

Lord, you are there when I'm lonely
I don't need to worry because you are with me
Lord, I learnt that you are everywhere
So when I am lonely
There's no need to fear.

47.

Bored

Dear Lord, I feel bored
I need some friends to play with
I know you love me
Please keep me company oh Lord
Let me feel your love and presence right now.
In Jesus' name I pray. Amen.

Chapter 5

Special Days Prayers

Birthday

48.

A new born baby
What a special gift from God
A new life to hold, cuddle and cherish
A new being so lovely, cute and precious
A bundle of joy we have waited for so long
Thank you Lord for this new born baby
May you keep, bless and be always near
Our new born baby, a precious gift from You.

49.

My birthday
Thank you, Lord, for this special day
It is not too long ago that I marked my last birthday
Thank you for all my gifts and good birthday wishes
Thank you for keeping me in the past years, dear Lord
Please be with me and bless me as I start another year
May I grow in wisdom, intelligence and understanding in Jesus' name.
Thank you, Lord, for this special day.

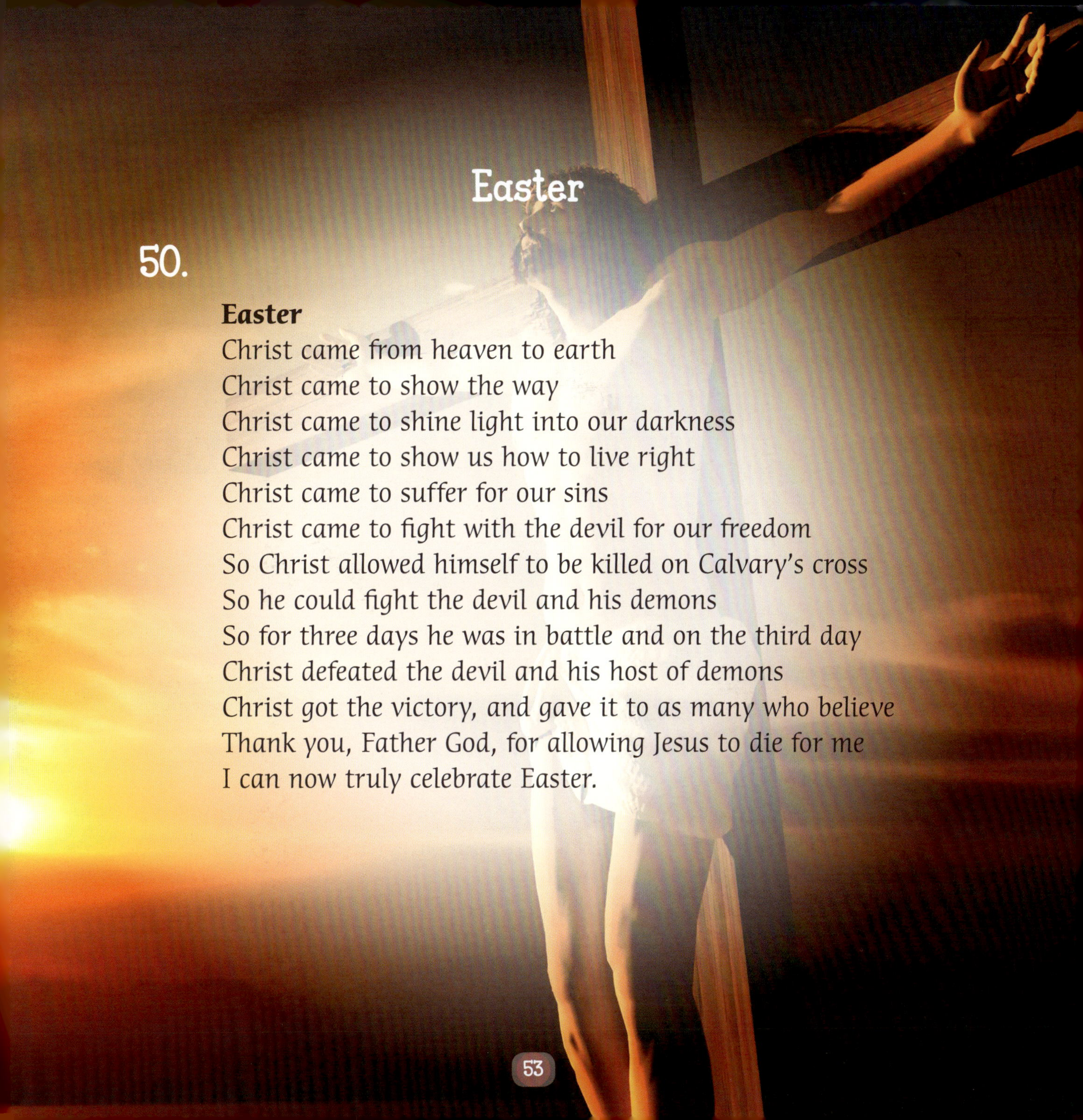

Easter

50.

Easter
Christ came from heaven to earth
Christ came to show the way
Christ came to shine light into our darkness
Christ came to show us how to live right
Christ came to suffer for our sins
Christ came to fight with the devil for our freedom
So Christ allowed himself to be killed on Calvary's cross
So he could fight the devil and his demons
So for three days he was in battle and on the third day
Christ defeated the devil and his host of demons
Christ got the victory, and gave it to as many who believe
Thank you, Father God, for allowing Jesus to die for me
I can now truly celebrate Easter.

Christmas

51.

This Christmas
This Christmas, may Christ be born in us
This Christmas, may joy be all around
This Christmas, may light shine into our darkness
This Christmas, may salvation be truly ours
This Christmas, may peace abound in all our hearts
This Christmas, may we have the best gift of all
Christ in us - the hope of glory
Thank you, Lord, for Christmas time.

52.

Christmas
Christmas time - lots of singing and carols
Christmas time - lots of gifts and good wishes
Christmas time - lots of food and parties
Christmas time - lots of bonding and family ties
Christmas time - lots of beautiful decorations and fun
Christmas time - lots of worship for a King who is born
Christmas time - may Christ be truly born in our hearts
Thank you, Father God, for Christmas
May the joy be all year round.

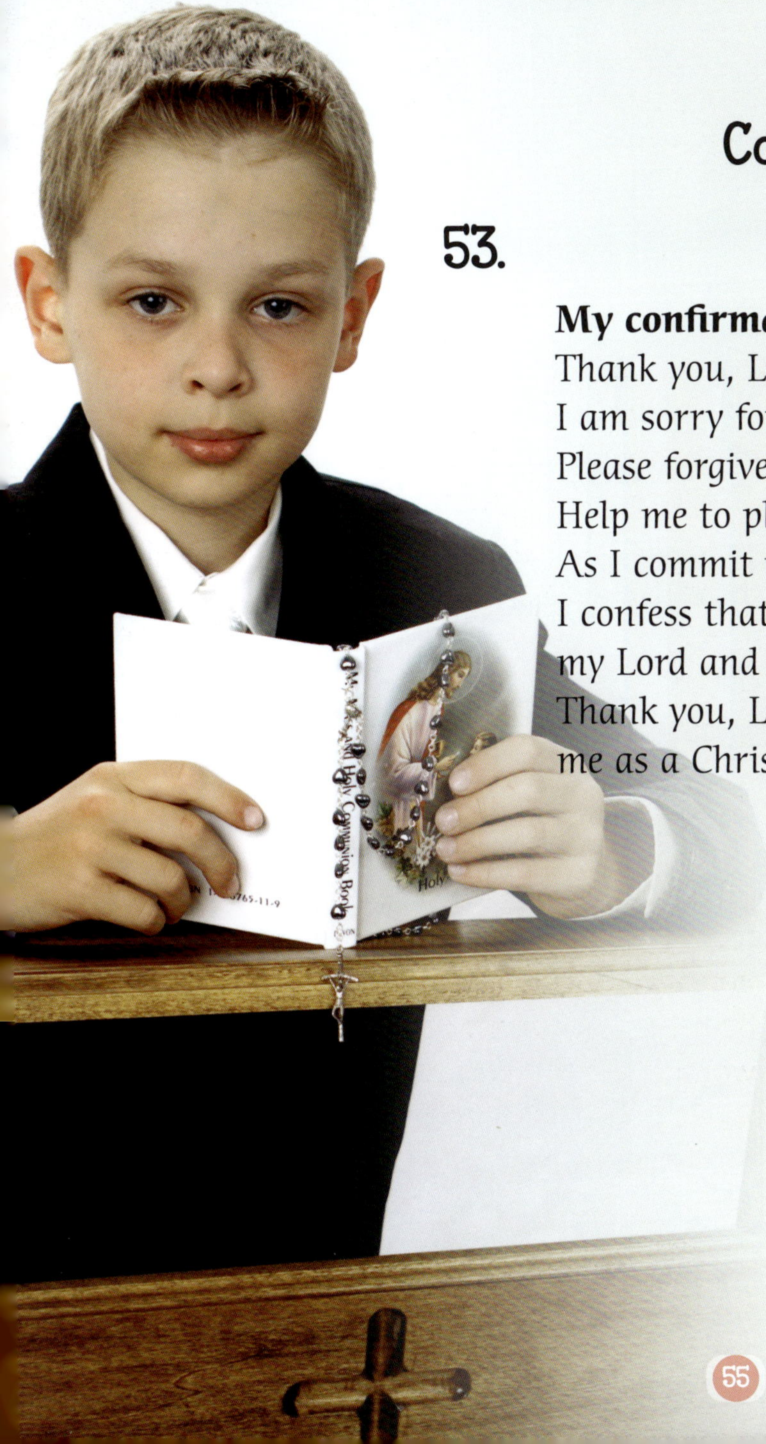

Confirmation

53.

My confirmation
Thank you, Lord, for saving me
I am sorry for all my wrongdoing
Please forgive me for all my wrongdoing
Help me to please you in all my ways from today
As I commit my life to serving you today
I confess that I believe in Jesus and that he is
my Lord and saviour.
Thank you, Lord, for saving me and accepting
me as a Christian.

Chapter 6

Prayers For Others

Children

54.

Children of the world

Lord Jesus, you said let the little children come to you
You must really love us because we can be noisy and naughty
Yet you said "Let the little children come to me"
Please bless all the little children of the world
Let them know your love and kindness
Be the father to the fatherless and mother to the motherless
To orphans, please be their parents,
To the needy, please meet their needs
To the hungry, provide food for them
To the sad and poor, please make them happy and rich
Father God, please bless all the children of the world
In Jesus' name I pray. Amen.

55.

That lonely child

Lord, I've heard of children in war-torn lands
I've heard of children who do not have food to eat
I've heard of children with no clothes to wear
Nor shoes for their feet
I've heard of children suffering and crying
Oh Lord, please help these children and give them a good life
In Jesus' mighty name I pray.

Friends

56.

My friends and I

Thank you, Lord, for the gift of friends
Someone to talk to
Someone to play with
Someone to share with
Someone to laugh with
This world is better because of good friends
Thank you, Lord, for the gifts of friends
Please bless all my friends in Jesus' name. Amen.

School

57.

My school
A place to learn
A place to play
A place of love, peace and friendship
Thank you, Lord, for all my friends and teachers
May your love and peace continue to be with us.

58.

My teacher
Thank you Lord for my teacher
For all he is teaching us so that we'll be great in life
Thank you Lord for all his time, patience and hard work
Please bless him and his family in Jesus ' name.

59.

The place I go to learn

Let your blessings be on my school
I love my school, the teachers, classmates and friends
I love the lessons - Maths, English, Science and Sports
I love lunch-time break and my yummy school dinner
I love all activities, school trips and the fun we all have together
Lord, please let your blessing be on my school, the teachers and the pupils
Be with us and keep us from all evil, give us wisdom and make us obedient children
In Jesus' name. Amen.

Chapter 7
Other Prayers

Christian Worship

60.

A wonderful book

How wonderful to be guided in doing right
By this precious gift called the Bible
Lots of interesting stories and lessons to learn
Lots of promisesof what God can do
How brilliant to have such a wonderful book
To guide and bless me every day.

61.

The place I go to worship

My church - I look forward to going every time
My church - place of warmth, love and friendship
My church - place of praise, prayer and worship
My church - place of learning, fun and snacking
My church - a wonderful place I always long to be
God bless my church, the pastor and Sunday school teachers
God bless all my friends and me as well
May we grow in your love and blessings, in Jesus' name.

61.

Alleluyah

Alleluyah, my very first church word
Alleluyah, I learnt is the heavenly language
Alleluyah, all praise to God
When I am grateful, I can say Alleluyah
When I am thankful, I can say Alleluyah
Even when I'm sad, I should say Alleluyah
Alleluyah, Alleluyah, must be a word you like, oh Lord
Alleluyah to you, oh Lord.

63.

Heaven

Heaven - most beautiful place ever seen
Heaven - happy singing all day long
Heaven - a place with streets of gold
Heaven - a place where angels live
Heaven - a place so peaceful and pure
Heaven - a place of godliness, love and wonders
Heaven - a place with many big houses
Dear Lord, let me make it to heaven, in Jesus' name.

Intimate Prayers

64.

Precious moments
Prayer time is one of my precious moments
God's peace, love and forgiveness are always present
In my precious moment of prayer
Precious moments - wonderful moments
Lord, let me always honour you at all times
Having precious moments with you throughout the day.

65.

Prayer of silence
Lord, thank you that I can talk to you
Sometimes all my friends are gone
And I'm left alone
But you are always there
Keeping me company and telling me
what to do
Bless my friends, my family, teachers
and neighbours
Bless me now as I pray to you in silence
and in Jesus' name.

66.

Amazing grace
Grace is favour I do not deserve
Yet you pour your grace on me anyway
I sometimes lie, fight and I'm often naughty
Then I ask for forgiveness, I say I'm sorry
And you always forgive me - just like that!
I enjoy your love and kindness - amazing grace!

67.

Quiet time
Morning time is quiet time
Quiet time is time with God
Time to read His words and hear Him speak
Time to sing praises to His name
Time to pray and be at peace
Time of instruction and understanding
Quiet time! Make it a special moment for me.

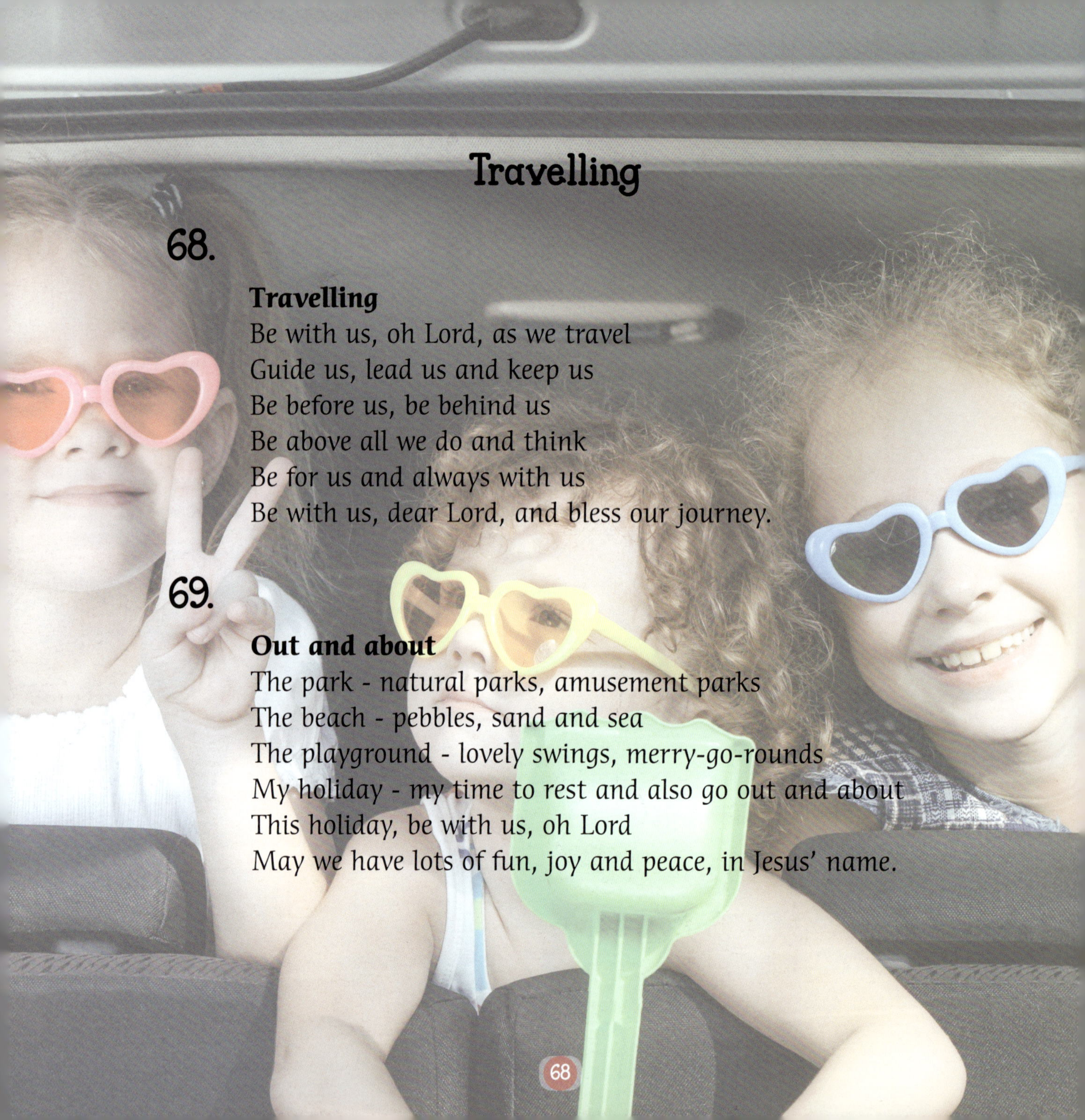

Travelling

68.

Travelling

Be with us, oh Lord, as we travel
Guide us, lead us and keep us
Be before us, be behind us
Be above all we do and think
Be for us and always with us
Be with us, dear Lord, and bless our journey.

69.

Out and about

The park - natural parks, amusement parks
The beach - pebbles, sand and sea
The playground - lovely swings, merry-go-rounds
My holiday - my time to rest and also go out and about
This holiday, be with us, oh Lord
May we have lots of fun, joy and peace, in Jesus' name.

Peace

70.

Peace
Grant us peace, oh Lord
Let there be peace in troubled neighbourhoods
Let there be peace in troubled cities
Let there be peace in troubled nations
Let there be peace among brothers and sisters
Let there be peace in my school and among my friends
Oh Lord, let there be your perfect peace that calms the storm
In Jesus' holy name I pray. Amen.

Sickness

71.

In sickness and in pain
Dear Lord, I learnt that you can do all things
You can help, heal, comfort and encourage
I am not feeling OK right now
Please help, heal, comfort and encourage me
In Jesus' name I pray. Amen.

72.

Jesus heals

Jesus, you healed the official's son
Jesus, you healed Peter's mother-in-law
Jesus, you healed the widow of Nain's son
Jesus, you healed Jairus' daughter from death
Jesus, you healed the ten people with leprous skin
Jesus, you healed so many people, as recorded in the Holy Book
Please heal me as I pray in your name. Amen.

73.

Feeling poorly

Dear Lord,
I don't feel like eating, I've no interest in food
I don't feel strong, although I would love to play
I feel like crying, kind of a little bit sore
As I lie in bed, please be with me
Heal me and surround me with your love
Bless me now and all the people taking care of me.

Bible Verses about Prayers

If you believe, you will receive whatever you ask for in prayer.
Matthew 21:22 NIV

The eyes of the Lord watch over those who do right, and his ears are open to their prayers. But the Lord turns his face against those who do evil. 1 Peter 3:12 NLT

Keep on asking, and you will receive what you ask for. Keep on seeking, and you will find. Keep on knocking, and the door will be opened to you.
Matthew 7:7 NLT

You can ask for anything in my name, and I will do it, so that the Son can bring glory to the Father. John 14:13 NLT

The Lord is far from the wicked, but he hears the prayers of the righteous.
Proverbs 15:29 NLT

In those days when you pray, I will listen. If you look for me wholeheartedly, you will find me. Jeremiah 29:12 NLT

I will answer them before they even call to me. While they are still talking about their needs, I will go ahead and answer their prayers!
Isaiah 65:24 NLT

Never stop praying. 1 Thessalonians 5:17 NLT

Index of Themes

About the Author

Dr Foyeke Christiana Tolani assists her husband in pastoring Christ's Love Assembly, a parish of The Redeemed Christian Church of God (RCCG) in Oxford, UK. She holds a PhD in Microbiology, a Masters in Public Health and an Advanced Diploma in Ministry. Foyeke has lived in and visited over 20 countries in different parts of the world and currently works as a Global Humanitarian Public Health Specialist. She used to lecture at the University of Lagos, Nigeria and has taught courses related to Disaster Relief at various universities in the USA and UK.

Dr Tolani, together with her husband, coordinates and co -presents a TV and web-based devotional programme called 'Open Heavens Reflections' on Sky channel 199. This is based on the devotional writings of the General Overseer of the Redeemed Christian Church of God, Pastor E.A. Adeboye. She has been privileged to preach, be blessed and be a blessing in countries throughout Europe and Africa.

Other Publications by the Author

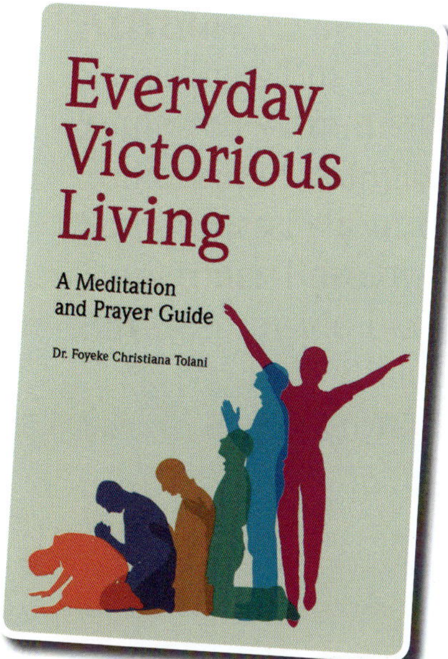

Book

Gospel Tracts

Contemporary, yet powerful life transforming evangelism tracts and icebreakers

For purchase and enquiries visit **www.publicisejesus.com** or write **admin@publicisejesus.org** or call **07405840935**.